Measuring with Fractions

Nancy Harris

Publishing LLC
Vero Beach, Florida 32964

www.rourkepublishing.com

PHOTO CREDITS: © Krista Mackey: title page, page 4; © Tom Young: page 4; © Jolande Gerritsen: page 7; © Bill Grove: page 8, 11; © Chris Scredon: page 9; © Amy Myers: page 12, 20; © David Edwards: page 13; © Amanda Rohde: page 17; © Christine Balderas: page 19; © Duc Do: page 21; © Rick Hyman: page 22.

Editor: Robert Stengard-Olliges

Cover design by Nicola Stratford, bdpublishing.com

Library of Congress Cataloging-in-Publication Data

Harris, Nancy
  Is an inchworm an inch? : measuring with fractions / Nancy Harris.
     p. cm.
  Includes index.
  ISBN 978-1-60044-645-0 (Hardcover)
  ISBN 978-1-60044-689-4 (Softcover)
  1. Fractions--Juvenile literature. I. Title.

  QA117.H39 2008
  513.2'6--dc22

                              2007018143

Printed in the USA

CG/CG

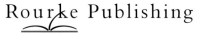

Rourke Publishing

www.rourkepublishing.com – rourke@rourkepublishing.com
Post Office Box 3328, Vero Beach, FL 32964

Table of Contents

Inchworms and Football   4

The Football Field   6

Halftime   14

Fourth Quarter   20

Glossary   23

Index   24

Inchworms and Football

Two of David's favorite things were playing **football** and bugs, especially inchworms. David admired how much effort an inchworm put into moving. Scrunch, stretch, move one **inch**!

David thought an inchworm's movement and playing football were a lot alike. It can take a lot of effort to move the football just one inch.

The Football Field

In football, measurement is very important. A football field looks like a huge **ruler**.

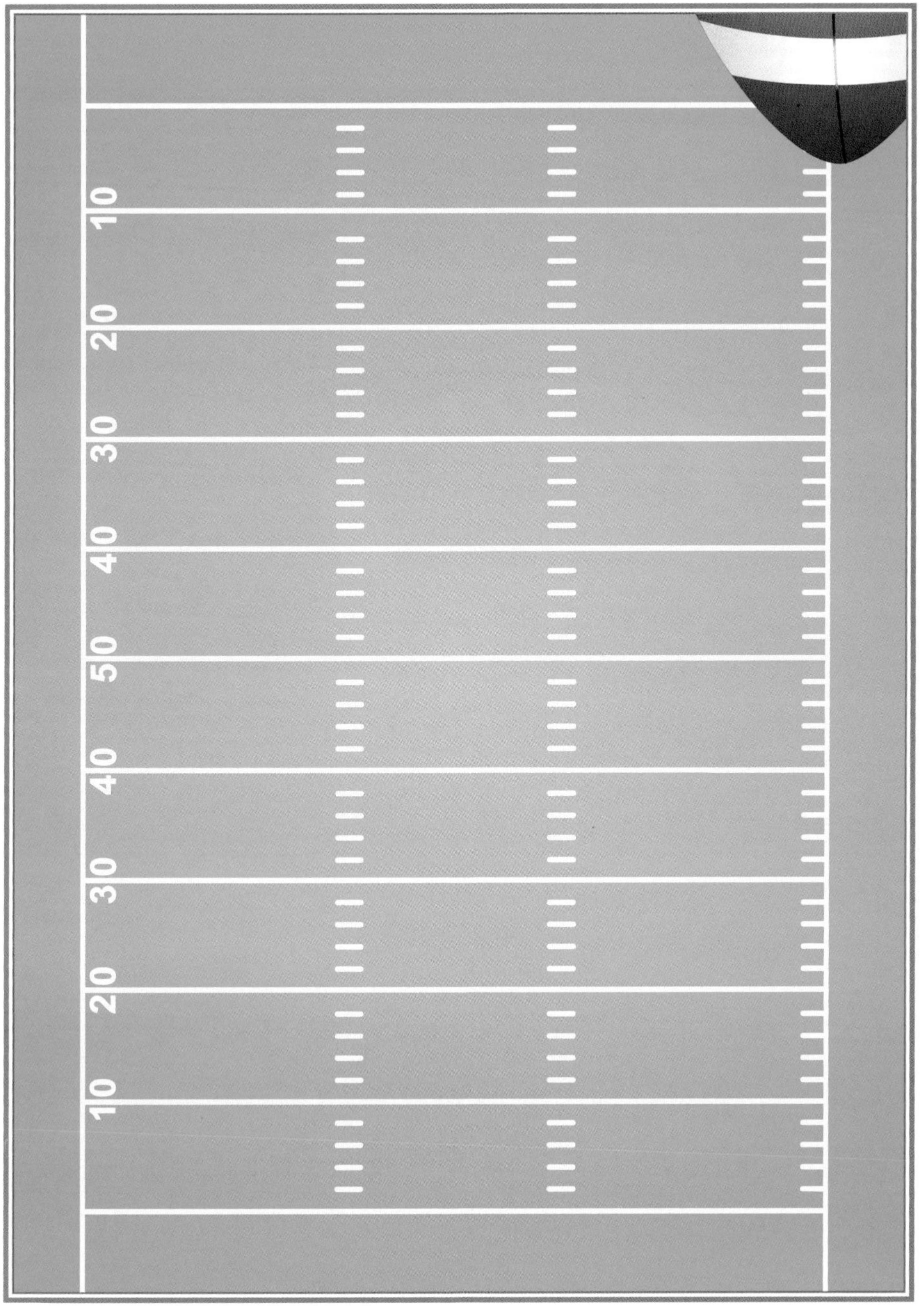
10
20
30
40
50
40
30
20
10

David knows his team has to move the football 10 **yards** for every first down. He wondered how many times an inchworm would have to scrunch and stretch to move 10 yards.

36 inches (1 yard)
x 10 yards
360 inches

Answer: There are 360 inches (or scrunches and stretches) in 10 yards!

Since the football doesn't always land on a line, football referees use a special tool called a **chain set** to mark and measure the distance the football moves.

chain

David remembers one game where his team really needed a first down so they could kick a field goal before halftime.

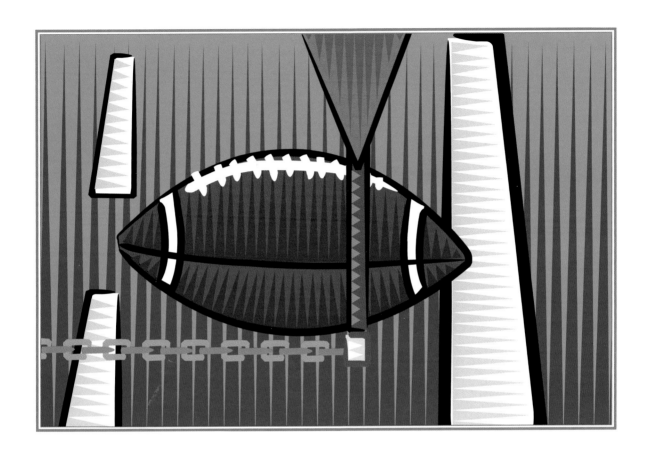

After the third down, the referees used the
chain set to measure how far the ball moved.
The ball had moved about two inches past
the end of the chain. FIRST DOWN!

Halftime

A football game is **divided** into four quarters. Halftime is in the middle of a game between the 2nd and 3rd quarters.

Quarter	Length	Amount of game completed at end of quarter
1st Quarter	15 Minutes	1/4 of the game
2nd Quarter	15 Minutes	2/4 or 1/2 of the game
Halftime		
3rd Quarter	15 Minutes	3/4 of the game
4th Quarter	15 Minutes	4/4 or 1 whole game

David's mom, dad, sister, and uncle always come to his games. At halftime, they always buy a pizza cut into eight slices. Everyone eats two slices. What **fraction** of the pizza does each person eat?

Each persons gets 2/8 or 1/4 of the pizza.

At one game, David's dad had $12.00 left to buy drinks. He bought two drinks for $4.00. What fraction of the $12.00 did he have left at the end of halftime?

David's dad had 8/12 or 2/3 of his money left after buying two drinks.

Fourth Quarter

In one game, time was running out in the fourth quarter. The score was tied 7 – 7. David was trying to run the ball for a touchdown but got tackled. The referee held his hands up about three inches apart showing how close the ball was to the goal line.

3 inches

On the next play, David got the ball again and this time he thought about the inchworm, scrunch, stretch, scrunch, S T R E T C H! As David was tackled, he stretched one more time. TOUCHDOWN!

David's team won 14 - 7. That's double the
points of the other team.

Glossary

chain set (CHAYN SET) — a unit of measure in football, a chain set has two poles with a 10 yard chain in between

divide (duh VIDE) — to break something up into parts

football (FUT bal) — a game played by two teams on a long field with goals on either end

fraction (FRAK shuhn) — a part of a whole number, such as 1/2, 2/3, 7/8

inch (INCH) — a unit of measure equal to 1/12 of a foot

ruler (ROO lur) — a tool for measuring

yard (YARD) — a unit of measure, a yard is three feet or 36 inches long

Index

football   4, 5, 6, 8, 10
fraction   16, 18
halftime   12, 14, 15, 16, 18
inch   4, 5, 9, 13, 20
inchworms   4, 5, 8, 21

measure   6, 10, 13
quarter   14, 15, 20
ruler   6
yards   8, 9

Further Reading

Dodds, Dayle. Full House: *An Invitation to Fractions*. Candlewick Press, 2007.

Pistoia, Sara. *Fractions*. Child's World, 2007.

Townsend, Donna. *Apple Fractions*. Children's Press, 2004.

Recommended Websites

www.funbrain.com/measure
www.funbrain.com/fract
www.kidsolr.com/math

About the Author

Nancy Harris is an educational consultant with twenty years teaching experience. She enjoys writing nonfiction books and teaching students and educators nonfiction reading strategies. She currently lives in Lafayette, Colorado.